ARCTIC
TALE

COMPANION TO THE MAJOR MOTION PICTURE

ARCTIC TALE

BY REBECCA BAINES
BASED ON THE MOTION PICTURE NARRATION
WRITTEN BY LINDA WOOLVERTON
AND MOSE RICHARDS AND KRISTIN GORE

NATIONAL GEOGRAPHIC
WASHINGTON, DC

Paperback ISBN: 978-1-4263-0084-4

Library edition ISBN: 978-1-4263-0085-1

Cataloging in Publication Data available upon request.

Photo credits: 1: Norbert Rosing / NGS; 2-3: Norbert Rosing/ NGS; 5: Paul Nicklen/ NGS;
6: Norbert Rosing/ NGS; 7: Paul Nicklen/ NGS 8 Norbert Rosing/ NGS; 9: Paul Nicklen/ NGS 10 up: Paul Nicklen/
NGS; 10 center: Norbert Rosing/ NGS 10 lo: Norbert Rosing/ NGS 11 all: Paul Nicklen/ NGS 12: Steve Kazlowski/
naturepl.com; 13: Ralph Lee Hopkins/NGS 14 all: Norbert Rosing/ NGS; 15: Goran Ehlme 16-17: Paul Nicklen/ NGS
18: Norbert Rosing/ NGS; 19: Ralph Lee Hopkins/ NGS; 20: Norbert Rosing/ NGS; 21: Norbert Rosing/ NGS;
22-23: Norbert Rosing/ NGS; 24: Tom Murphy/ NGS; 25: Norbert Rosing/ NGS; 26: Paul Nicklen/ NGS
27: Paul Nicklen/ NGS 28-29: Norbert Rosing/ NGS; 30-31: Paul Nicklen/ NGS 32 up: Norbert Rosing/ NGS
32 lo: Paul Nicklen/ NGS Back cover: Paul Nicklen/ NGS

One of the world's largest nonprofit scientific and educational organizations,
the National Geographic Society was founded in 1888 "for the increase and diffusion of
geographic knowledge." Fulfilling this mission, the Society educates and inspires millions every day
through its magazines, books, television programs, videos, maps and atlases, research grants,
the National Geographic Bee, teacher workshops, and innovative classroom materials.
The Society is supported through membership dues, charitable gifts,
and income from the sale of its educational products.
This support is vital to National Geographic's mission to increase global understanding
and promote conservation of our planet through exploration, research, and education.

For more information, please call
1-800-NGS-LINE (647-5463) or write to the following address:

NATIONAL GEOGRAPHIC SOCIETY

1145 17th Street N.W., Washington, D.C. 20036-4688 U.S.A.

Visit the Society's Web site: www.nationalgeographic.com

PRINTED IN U.S.A.

A REAL ADVENTURE
IN THE COOLEST PLACE ON EARTH

This is the Arctic—a giant stretch of solid ice at the very top of the globe. In the winter, the winds whip across the frozen landscape, and the temperature can reach 80 degrees below zero. It might not seem like a comfortable place for anyone, but it's spring and there are two new creatures about to call this icy world home.

Nanu is a baby polar bear just a few weeks old.
Until now she has known only the warm, dark
den her mother built for her before she was
born. But Nanu is ready to leave her cramped
cave and tumble down the hills of Snow
Mountain.

Seela is a newborn walrus. Her family lives far from Snow Mountain, past the edge of land where the ice meets the sea. She will spend most of her life in the water, but she needs the sturdy ice to rest on when she is too tired to swim.

Seela lives in a big family group—all female. There are dozens of sisters, aunts, and cousins for her to play with. Seela will always live with her family, no matter how big she gets.

Nanu will spend the next couple of years in the company of her mother, living the wandering life of a polar bear. They will go down to the ice shelf, not far from Seela's home, to hunt for seals. When Nanu is big enough, she will set out into the world to live on her own.

Nanu and Seela might have very different
families and ways of life, but they have a lot
in common, too.

Nanu eats...

Nanu sleeps...

Nanu plays...

Seela eats...

Seela sleeps...

And Seela plays.

Just like human babies, they have adults to care for them and teach them all they need to know.

Nanu's mother shows her how to hunt for seals, resting in snow burrows in the ice. She sniffs out her next meal then pounces on the spot where the seal is hidden.

It takes years of practice to surprise a slippery seal, but by the age of two Nanu has mastered this skill...

... so now it is time for
Nanu's mother to say goodbye.

The first thing Seela must learn
is how to pull her body up onto the ice.

Mom gives her a little shove,

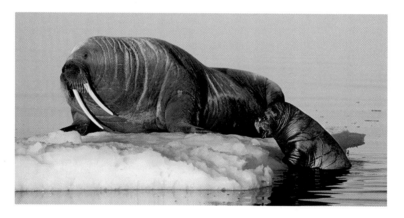

then waits patiently
as Seela tries to pull herself out of the water.

Mom rewards her with a well-deserved kiss.

When she is big enough, she learns how
hunt with the herd, preying on clams that rest
at the bottom of the ocean. Seela snuffles the
clams out of the dirt, blasts them open with a
snort, and sucks out the meat. A tiny clam may
not seem like much of a meal for a growing
walrus, but Seela can eat up to 4,000 of them
in a three-day feast.

Only two years have passed since they were born, but the home that Nanu and Seela know is melting. Times are changing for all Arctic animals. Every year, the temperature gets warmer and the summers longer. The hard sea ice breaks up earlier and re-forms later.

With the early arrival of summer, Seela has no place to rest her tired flippers…

And even worse, Nanu can't hunt seals the way her mother taught her. Without food, she will not last through the summer months when seals are hardest to find.

When their environment changes, all animals must adapt, or change the way they live. Sometimes this means finding a new home. Seela's family has experienced bad ice years in the past, and they remember an island with plenty of hard rocks where they can rest. It's a long swim, but they've got sleek bodies meant for gliding through water and plenty of blubber to keep them warm.

Driven by hunger, Nanu must leave too. The trip is harder for her because polar bears are not built for long-distance swimming. They are better swimmers than grizzly bears because they have webbed feet, and they have plenty of fat under their fur to keep them warm in the Arctic cold. But a 200-mile trip is still a lot to ask of a bear.

Luckily, Nanu finds some rest stops along the way.

After about a week of swimming, both Nanu and Seela arrive at Rock Island. Seela's family joins hundreds of other walruses that have also made the trip. It's not easy to pull themselves up so high when they're used to the sea and the ice, but they know their tired bodies need to rest. Eventually they take their places on the rocky earth.

When Nanu arrives, she is starving. She must find food, and fast. She tries to hunt on the island, but there are no seals here, and she is too small to hunt walrus. But there is another hungry animal lurking nearby, a big male polar bear. Males can be as much as three times the size of females and can go after larger prey. Luckily, Nanu convinces him to share his meal.

For the next six years, both Nanu and Seela
return to Rock Island for the summer. Each
fall, when the seasons change, an old walrus
sniffs the ice in the air, and the herd heads
home. When the walruses leave, Nanu knows her
icy kingdom has returned, and she embarks on
the tiring trip back. In their eighth year of life,
Nanu and Seela are full grown, and there is a new
sense of excitement about the journey home.

Nanu has found a mate and is ready have cubs
of her own. She climbs up Snow Mountain
and builds a den like the one where she was
born. There she waits.

Any male that wants Seela's attention is going to have to earn it! Male walruses sing love songs to attract a mate. When necessary, they can sing up to 40 hours! But sure enough, one determined male finally wins her over.

And in the spring, when the Arctic darkness fades, there are three new lives in the land of ice.

What does the Arctic have in store
for these new children of the north?
Only time will tell.